The God Really Loves You Book Series™ Presents:

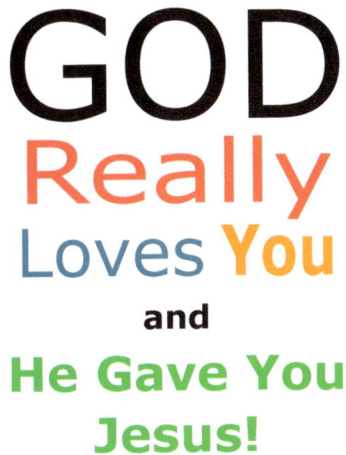

GOD
Really
Loves You
and
He Gave You Jesus!

**Written and Illustrated
by Wendy Nelson**

God Really Loves You Book Series™ presents:

GOD Really Loves You
and He Gave You Jesus!

Text Copyright ©2022 by Wendy Nelson
Artwork Copyright ©2022 by Wendy Nelson

Published by MediaTek Grafx
POB 62, Bonnieville, Kentucky, 42713

ISBN 978-1-0879-0060-5

Design and production by MediaTek Grafx, Bonnieville, Kentucky
Special thanks to Joan Swan for loving review, critique and advice

The Publisher has made every effort to avoid errors or omissions. Opinions, stories, and themes are intended for entertainment, motivation for research and future study. This book includes content that is non-fiction.

All Scripture quotations are from the The Holy Bible, King James Version, Pradis Software Rel 02.04.03, Built with Conform Version 5.00.0051, Version 5.1.50 Copyright ©2002 The Zondervan Corporation All Rights Reserved.

All rights reserved. This Publication may not be reproduced in whole or in part, stored or transmitted by any means. Media may use small portions for reviews. Please request written permission from Publisher for any other reason.

Printed in the United States of America

A Special Gift for

———————————

From

———————————

Note

————————————————

————————————————

————————————————

Date

———————————

God really loves you!
The Bible is the story of God's love for you!

God gave you the Bible,
to show you how to live,
and to tell you about
His Son, Jesus.

He loves you
this much!

1 John 4:19 We love him, because he first loved us.

1 John 3:1 Behold, what manner of love the Father hath bestowed upon us, that we should be called the sons of God: therefore the world knoweth us not, because it knew him not.

We try to always do good things,
but sometimes we do very bad things.
In the Bible, God says
those bad things are sin.

Sin is against God's rules.
If we take someone's
belongings, that is stealing.
If we love something
more than God, it is an idol.
If we are proud and bragging,
it is a sin.
If we are lying and not telling
the truth, it is a sin.
If we speak bad things about
other people or about God,
it is a sin.
If we don't forgive people,
it is a sin.

*Proverbs 20:11 Even a child is known by his doings,
whether his work be pure, and whether it be right.*

*1 John 3:4 Whosoever committeth sin transgresseth also
the law: for sin is the transgression of the law.*

*James 4:17 Therefore to him that knoweth to do good,
and doeth it not, to him it is sin.*

*Mark 7:21-22 For from within, out of the heart of men,
proceed evil thoughts, adulteries, fornications, murders, 22
Thefts, covetousness, wickedness, deceit, lasciviousness,
an evil eye, blasphemy, pride, foolishness:*

God cannot tolerate sin,
because God is Holy.

God wants
a relationship with you
and He loves you.

People need forgiveness
when they sin,
so they can have
a relationship
with God.

God tries to protect us.
He wants us to know that sin leads to death.
Sin is so awful, and as we grow up,
we should not do bad things.
We are not prefect, so we make mistakes
and we all do bad things.

*Romans 6:23 For the wages of sin is death;
but the gift of God is eternal life
through Jesus Christ our Lord.*

*Habakkuk 1:13 Thou art of purer eyes than to behold evil,
and canst not look on iniquity:*

We need God to forgive us.
In the Old Testament, in the Bible,
God told us that a sacrifice would pay
for our sins and make things right with God.

During the time of Moses the prophet,
God told people to sacrifice
an innocent animal to pay for their sins.

*Leviticus 1:1-3 And the LORD called unto Moses, and spake unto him out of the tabernacle of the congregation, saying, 2 Speak unto the children of Israel, and say unto them, If any man of you bring an offering unto the LORD, ye shall bring your offering of the cattle, even of the herd, and of the flock. 3 If his offering be a burnt sacrifice of the herd, let him offer a male without blemish:
he shall offer it of his own voluntary will at the door
of the tabernacle of the congregation before the LORD.*

A sacrifice is something highly valued that people gave to God, to show Him they were sorry for their sins.

A sacrifice would be like giving your favorite toy to God, to say that you are sorry, and that you love Him.

The people in the past chose one of their valuable animals for sacrifice.

They chose a perfect and innocent sheep, goat, ox, bull, pigeon or dove to sacrifice to God. People showed God how much they loved Him, by giving a sacrifice to Him.

Leviticus 4:1-3 And the LORD spake unto Moses, saying, 2 Speak unto the children of Israel, saying, If a soul shall sin through ignorance against any of the commandments of the LORD concerning things which ought not to be done, and shall do against any of them: 3 If the priest that is anointed do sin according to the sin of the people; then let him bring for his sin, which he hath sinned, a young bullock without blemish unto the LORD for a sin offering.

When an innocent animal
was killed for a sin offering sacrifice,
the people saw the blood, and felt so bad!
They knew they sinned and they were sorry.

The innocent animal died, instead of the people who were sinners!

God was pleased that the people were sorry and did not want to sin any more. God was pleased that people chose to love and obey Him!

Hebrews 9:22 And almost all things are by the law purged with blood; and without shedding of blood is no remission.

2 Chronicles 29:28 And all the congregation worshipped, and the singers sang, and the trumpeters sounded: and all this continued until the burnt offering was finished.

That was according to God's law in Biblical times, a long time ago.

In the New Testament, in the Bible, God had a plan for the future, for all mankind, to provide forgiveness for sin.

Romans 3:23-25 For all have sinned, and come short of the glory of God; 24 Being justified freely by his grace through the redemption that is in Christ Jesus: 25 Whom God hath set forth to be a propitiation through faith in his blood, to declare his righteousness for the remission of sins that are past, through the forbearance of God;

God wanted to provide a choice for people, so they could choose to feel sorry for their sins, to repent, and to be forgiven.

Then, when they are forgiven, they can have a relationship with their Father in Heaven! This was God's plan.

Romans 5:8-11 But God commendeth his love toward us, in that, while we were yet sinners, Christ died for us. 9 Much more then, being now justified by his blood, we shall be saved from wrath through him. 10 For if, when we were enemies, we were reconciled to God by the death of his Son, much more, being reconciled, we shall be saved by his life. 11 And not only so, but we also joy in God through our Lord Jesus Christ, by whom we have now received the atonement.

God sent the angel, Gabriel, to speak to a chosen, pure woman named Mary, from Nazareth.

The angel told Mary she would have a son by the Holy Spirit of God. It would be a miracle! The angel said Mary should name her son Jesus, or Yeshua in the Hebrew language.

The angel said Jesus is the Son of God, the Savior, the Messiah. God's name in Hebrew is Yahweh.

Matthew 1:21-23 And she shall bring forth a son, and thou shalt call his name JESUS: for he shall save his people from their sins. 22 Now all this was done, that it might be fulfilled which was spoken of the Lord by the prophet, saying, 23 Behold, a virgin shall be with child, and shall bring forth a son, and they shall call his name Emmanuel, which being interpreted is, God with us.

When Mary was ready to give birth,
she was travelling with Joseph,
and they arrived in Bethlehem.
There was no available room
in the guest chamber.
Jesus was born,
wrapped in swaddling clothes,
and laid in a manger,
by the animals.

It was a special day!
We love baby Jesus!

Christmas is the day we celebrate
the birth of Jesus.

Luke 2:6-7 And so it was, that, while they were there, the days were accomplished that she should be delivered. 7 And she brought forth her firstborn son, and wrapped him in swaddling clothes, and laid him in a manger; because there was no room for them in the inn.

An angel came to shepherds in nearby fields.

The angel told the shepherds to go see baby Jesus, the Savior!

Then, a multitude of angels of heaven appeared, and the shepherds prasied God!

Luke 2:9-14 And, lo, the angel of the Lord came upon them, and the glory of the Lord shone round about them: and they were sore afraid. 10 And the angel said unto them, Fear not: for, behold, I bring you good tidings of great joy, which shall be to all people. 11 For unto you is born this day in the city of David a Saviour, which is Christ the Lord. 12 And this shall be a sign unto you; Ye shall find the babe wrapped in swaddling clothes, lying in a manger. 13 And suddenly there was with the angel a multitude of the heavenly host praising God, and saying, 14 Glory to God in the highest, and on earth peace, good will toward men.

They followed the star, until they found Jesus.
They brought gifts to Jesus, born to be our Savior.

Matthew 2:9-11 When they had heard the king, they departed; and, lo, the star, which they saw in the east, went before them, till it came and stood over where the young child was. 10 When they saw the star, they rejoiced with exceeding great joy. 11 And when they were come into the house, they saw the young child with Mary his mother, and fell down, and worshipped him: and when they had opened their treasures, they presented unto him gifts; gold, and frankincense, and myrrh.

As Jesus grew up, as a boy,
He went to the temple, speaking to teachers.

When Jesus was a man,
He started His ministry.
He was teaching everyone about God!

Luke 2:46 And it came to pass, that after three days they found him in the temple, sitting in the midst of the doctors, both hearing them, and asking them questions.

Luke 2:49 And he said unto them, How is it that ye sought me? wist ye not that I must be about my Father's business?

Matthew 4:17-19 From that time Jesus began to preach, and to say, Repent: for the kingdom of heaven is at hand. 18 And Jesus, walking by the sea of Galilee, saw two brethren, Simon called Peter, and Andrew his brother, casting a net into the sea: for they were fishers. 19 And he saith unto them, Follow me, and I will make you fishers of men.

Mark 1:8-11 I indeed have baptized you with water: but he shall baptize you with the Holy Ghost.
9 And it came to pass in those days, that Jesus came from Nazareth of Galilee, and was baptized of John in Jordan.
10 And straightway coming up out of the water, he saw the heavens opened, and the Spirit like a dove descending upon him:
11 And there came a voice from heaven, saying, Thou art my beloved Son, in whom I am well pleased.

Jesus travelled to many villages, healing people, teaching, and performing miracles.

So many people were taught through parables, or stories, and given commandments. They learned about Jesus and about God, our Father in Heaven!

Matthew 4:23-24 And Jesus went about all Galilee, teaching in their synagogues, and preaching the gospel of the kingdom, and healing all manner of sickness and all manner of disease among the people. 24 And his fame went throughout all Syria: and they brought unto him all sick people that were taken with divers diseases and torments, and those which were possessed with devils, and those which were lunatick, and those that had the palsy; and he healed them.

Jesus taught the 12 apostles.
The apostles learned to minister, and to be obedient to God. Jesus taught people to pray, and to love their neighbors.

Mark 3:14 And he ordained twelve, that they should be with him, and that he might send them forth to preach,

Matthew 7:29 For he taught them as one having authority, and not as the scribes.

Luke 11:2-4 And he said unto them, When ye pray, say, Our Father which art in heaven, Hallowed be thy name. Thy kingdom come. Thy will be done, as in heaven, so in earth. 3 Give us day by day our daily bread. 4 And forgive us our sins; for we also forgive every one that is indebted to us. And lead us not into temptation; but deliver us from evil.

Jesus taught that we can love God or we can love money, but we can't love both.

OR

Jesus calmed the waters, healed people from diseases, performed miracles, and He brought people back to life!

Jesus corrected the leaders of churches.

Matthew 6:24 No man can serve two masters: for either he will hate the one, and love the other; or else he will hold to the one, and despise the other. Ye cannot serve God and mammon.

Luke 18:42 And Jesus said unto him, Receive thy sight: thy faith hath saved thee.

John 11:43-45 And when he thus had spoken, he cried with a loud voice, Lazarus, come forth. 44 And he that was dead came forth, bound hand and foot with graveclothes: and his face was bound about with a napkin. Jesus saith unto them, Loose him, and let him go. 45 Then many of the Jews which came to Mary, and had seen the things which Jesus did, believed on him.

Jesus appointed 70 more helpers to go two-by-two to all of the villages in advanvce, before Jesus.

Luke 10:1 After these things the Lord appointed other seventy also, and sent them two and two before his face into every city and place, whither he himself would come.

Ephesians 2:8-10 For by grace are ye saved through faith; and that not of yourselves: it is the gift of God: 9 Not of works, lest any man should boast. 10 For we are his workmanship, created in Christ Jesus unto good works, which God hath before ordained that we should walk in them.

Luke 10:20 Notwithstanding in this rejoice not, that the spirits are subject unto you; but rather rejoice, because your names are written in heaven.

One of the 12 apostles, Judas, betrayed Jesus for 30 pieces of silver. Jesus was arrested and taken to the governor.

Jesus was innocent! The governor didn't feel Jesus committed any crime, and asked an angry mob of people to choose who should live. Of the two who were arrested, as it was their custom, the angry mob of people chose. They chose the criminal Barabbas to live.

John 18:2-3 And Judas also, which betrayed him, knew the place: for Jesus ofttimes resorted thither with his disciples. 3 Judas then, having received a band of men and officers from the chief priests and Pharisees, cometh thither with lanterns and torches and weapons.

John 18:12 Then the band and the captain and officers of the Jews took Jesus, and bound him,

John 18:39-40 But ye have a custom, that I should release unto you one at the passover: will ye therefore that I release unto you the King of the Jews? 40 Then cried they all again, saying, Not this man, but Barabbas. Now Barabbas was a robber.

Jesus was severely beaten, they put a crown of thorns on His head, and He was forced to carry His cross through the city streets. In those times, criminals were crucified.

Jesus was innocent, but He willingly gave His life, and He was nailed to a cross to die, between two guilty criminals. Good Friday is the day that Jesus gave His life for our sins.

John 19:1-2 Then Pilate therefore took Jesus, and scourged him. 2 And the soldiers platted a crown of thorns, and put it on his head, and they put on him a purple robe,

John 19:17-18 And he bearing his cross went forth into a place called the place of a skull, which is called in the Hebrew Golgotha: 18 Where they crucified him, and two other with him, on either side one, and Jesus in the midst.

1 Timothy 2:3-5 For this is good and acceptable in the sight of God our Saviour; 4 Who will have all men to be saved, and to come unto the knowledge of the truth. 5 For there is one God, and one mediator between God and men, the man Christ Jesus;

Don't worry. This true story has a good ending!

After Jesus died on the cross, they put His body in a tomb that was sealed with a huge rock in front of the opening, and they guarded it.

Three days later, Mary went to the tomb and it was open! The angel told Mary that Jesus wasn't there.
Then, Mary spoke to Jesus!

On the third day, **Jesus arose from the dead**! Easter is the day that Jesus was resurrected. Jesus conqured sin and death. Jesus is alive!

Matthew 27:60 And laid it in his own new tomb, which he had hewn out in the rock: and he rolled a great stone to the door of the sepulchre, and departed.

Matthew 27:66 So they went, and made the sepulchre sure, sealing the stone, and setting a watch.

Matthew 28:5-7 And the angel answered and said unto the women, Fear not ye: for I know that ye seek Jesus, which was crucified. 6 He is not here: for he is risen, as he said. Come, see the place where the Lord lay. 7 And go quickly, and tell his disciples that he is risen from the dead; and, behold, he goeth before you into Galilee; there shall ye see him: lo, I have told you.

After that, 500 more people saw Jesus!

Jesus also went to speak to the apostles.

They were told to teach the good news, or the Gospel, of God's salvation plan through Jesus!

1 Corinthians 15:6 After that, he was seen of above five hundred brethren at once; of whom the greater part remain unto this present, but some are fallen asleep.

Matthew 28:16-20 Then the eleven disciples went away into Galilee, into a mountain where Jesus had appointed them. 17 And when they saw him, they worshipped him: but some doubted. 18 And Jesus came and spake unto them, saying, All power is given unto me in heaven and in earth. 19 Go ye therefore, and teach all nations, baptizing them in the name of the Father, and of the Son, and of the Holy Ghost:

Mark 16:15 And he said unto them, Go ye into all the world, and preach the gospel to every creature.

After 40 days with people, Jesus arose to Heaven, to the right hand of God!

As Jesus promised, 49 days after Easter, on Pentecost, the Holy Spirit came to live inside people who believe in Jesus!

The Holy Spirit is our comforter, teacher, and so much more. With the Holy Spirit we are never alone!

Jesus told us He will come back again, and we will live with Him, in Heaven, forever. Heaven is a beautiful place with God!

Mark 16:19 So then after the Lord had spoken unto them, he was received up into heaven, and sat on the right hand of God.

Acts 2:4 And they were all filled with the Holy Ghost, and began to speak with other tongues, as the Spirit gave them utterance.

Acts 1:11 Which also said, Ye men of Galilee, why stand ye gazing up into heaven? this same Jesus, which is taken up from you into heaven, shall so come in like manner as ye have seen him go into heaven.

We are forgiven, if we pray that we are sorry and turn away from our sin, and we accept Jesus as our Savior! We ask the Holy Spirit to come and live in us!

Then, we are saved by grace, God's love, and go to heaven when we die.

If we don't accept Jesus as our Savior, we are not forgiven for our sins, and we go to a firey place called hell when we die.

All innocent babies go to heaven, but we can choose to love Jesus, now! We want to grow up learning about and loving God, the Holy Spirit, and His Son, Jesus.

Acts 4:12 Neither is there salvation in any other: for there is none other name under heaven given among men, whereby we must be saved.

Ephesians 2:8-10 For by grace are ye saved through faith; and that not of yourselves: it is the gift of God: 9 Not of works, lest any man should boast. 10 For we are his workmanship, created in Christ Jesus unto good works, which God hath before ordained that we should walk in them.

Matthew 18:14 Even so it is not the will of your Father which is in heaven, that one of these little ones should perish.

We want to always repent
of any sins we do,
to be sorry,
and to stop those sins,
to ask God for forgiveness,
and to always love
Jesus and God.

Jesus said He is
coming back for us!

One day, everyone will see
Him coming
in the clouds above us!
He will bring us up to Him!

Until Jesus returns, we study the Bible, love God, love Jesus, and love our neighbors!
We can tell everyone about Jesus!
Maybe they will love Jesus, too!

1 Thessalonians 4:16-17 For the Lord himself shall descend from heaven with a shout, with the voice of the archangel, and with the trump of God: and the dead in Christ shall rise first: 17 Then we which are alive and remain shall be caught up together with them in the clouds, to meet the Lord in the air: and so shall we ever be with the Lord.

Matthew 22:37-39 Jesus said unto him, Thou shalt love the Lord thy God with all thy heart, and with all thy soul, and with all thy mind. 38 This is the first and great commandment. 39 And the second is like unto it, Thou shalt love thy neighbour as thyself.

Revelation 22:12 And, behold, I come quickly; and my reward is with me, to give every man according as his work shall be.

It was God's plan for Jesus to die for us.
Jesus was the sacrifice for our sins.

God gave us His Son, Jesus,
to pay for our sins,
so we can live and be close to God!

Jesus loves all little children!

John 3:16-17 For God so loved the world, that he gave his only begotten Son, that whosoever believeth in him should not perish, but have everlasting life. 17 For God sent not his Son into the world to condemn the world; but that the world through him might be saved.

Mark 10:14-16 But when Jesus saw it, he was much displeased, and said unto them, Suffer the little children to come unto me, and forbid them not: for of such is the kingdom of God. 15 Verily I say unto you, Whosoever shall not receive the kingdom of God as a little child, he shall not enter therein. 16 And he took them up in his arms, put his hands upon them, and blessed them.

JESUS	CHILDREN	HOLY SPIRIT
GOD	OLD TESTAMENT (39 books)	GOOD FRIDAY
REPENT	APOSTLES	AROSE
PENTECOST	CHRISTMAS	SACRIFICE

God Really Loves You Book Series™

GodReallyLovesYou.com

John 3:16-18 For God so loved the world, that he gave his only begotten Son, that whosoever believeth in him should not perish, but have everlasting life. 17 For God sent not his Son into the world to condemn the world; but that the world through him might be saved.
18 He that believeth on him is not condemned: but he that believeth not is condemned already, because he hath not believed in the name of the only begotten Son of God.

Matthew 18:3-5 And said, Verily I say unto you, Except ye be converted, and become as little children, ye shall not enter into the kingdom of heaven. Whosoever therefore shall humble himself as this little child, the same is greatest in the kingdom of heaven. And whoso shall receive one such little child in my name receiveth me.

www.ingramcontent.com/pod-product-compliance
Lightning Source LLC
Chambersburg PA
CBHW040122170426
42811CB00124B/1484